W9-BIB-837

OUTDOOR PUZZLES

HIGHLIGHTS PRESS

Honesdale, Pennsylvania

Welcome, Hidden Pictures® Puzzlers!

When you finish a puzzle, check it off √ . Good luck, and happy puzzling!

Contents

Cover Illustration by Chuck Dil

Crazy Race

flashlight

sailboat

ladle

golf club

doughnut

spider

dog bone

boot

tack

slice of pie

slice of bread

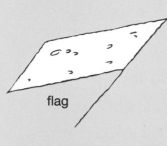

flag

caterpillar

banana

spoon

snow cone

nail

candle

open book

fishho

4

kite

bird

snake

broccoli

pointy hat

fish

carrot

slice of pizza

trowel

fork

closed umbrella

wrench

artist's brush

gravy boat

mug

sheep

Illustrated by Chuck Dillon

5

Portrait Day

handbell

heart

ice-cream bar

slice of pizza

mallet

crescent moon

saltshaker

needle

mug

banana

spool of thread

crown

snail

pencil

seashell

wishbone

worm

fork

Illustrated by Maggie Swanson

slice of lemon

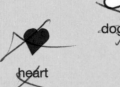
worm

heart

dog bone

mouse

slice of pizza

baseball bat

envelope

banana

open book

flag

domino

Walking the Dogs

Illustrated by Ethan Long

Dive In!

drinking glass

slice of pizza

bell

lemon wedge

screw

feather

shuttlecock

envelope

artist's brush

slice of pie

banana

crown

Illustrated by David Helton

Saturday Market

fishhook

pencil

musical note

mushroom

cowbell

dragonfly

megaphone

ring

crescent moon

nail

golf club

slice of pie

pushpin

goose

sailboat

drinking straw

candle

chicken

Illustrated by Linda Weller

Balloon Fest

heart

candle

radish

snail

funnel

artist's brush

shovel

musical note

trowel

coat hanger

moth

fork

eyeglasses

spoon

crescent moon

mushroom

wishbone

2 tacks

wrench

pennant

crown

needle

golf club

mug

worm

spatula

pear

key

comb

mitten

handbell

apple

ring

toothbrush

strawberry

olive

boomerang

muffin

flashlight

chef's hat

fishhook

light bulb

Illustrated by Larry Daste

11

Sea Turtle

sea horse

sailboat

anchor

bobber

oar

swim fin

fishhook

clamshell

submarine

sea gull

rowboat

ray

whale

eel

fish

shark

snail

Illustrated by Joe Seldita

12

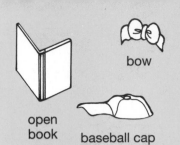
open
book

bow

baseball cap

flashlight

lima bean

ice-cream
bar

popcorn

domino

slice of bread

broccoli

pot
holder

Don't Look!

green
bean

teacup

mitten

stalk of
celery

harmonica

tape
dispenser

lollipop

clamshell

Illustrated by Susan Dahlman

13

Arbor Day

carrot

worm

bell

whisk broom

baseball bat

pennant

slice of bread

crown

muffin

acorn

book

camera

sailboat

canoe

bird

handbag

14

Illustrated by Susan Dahlman

Bumperdillos

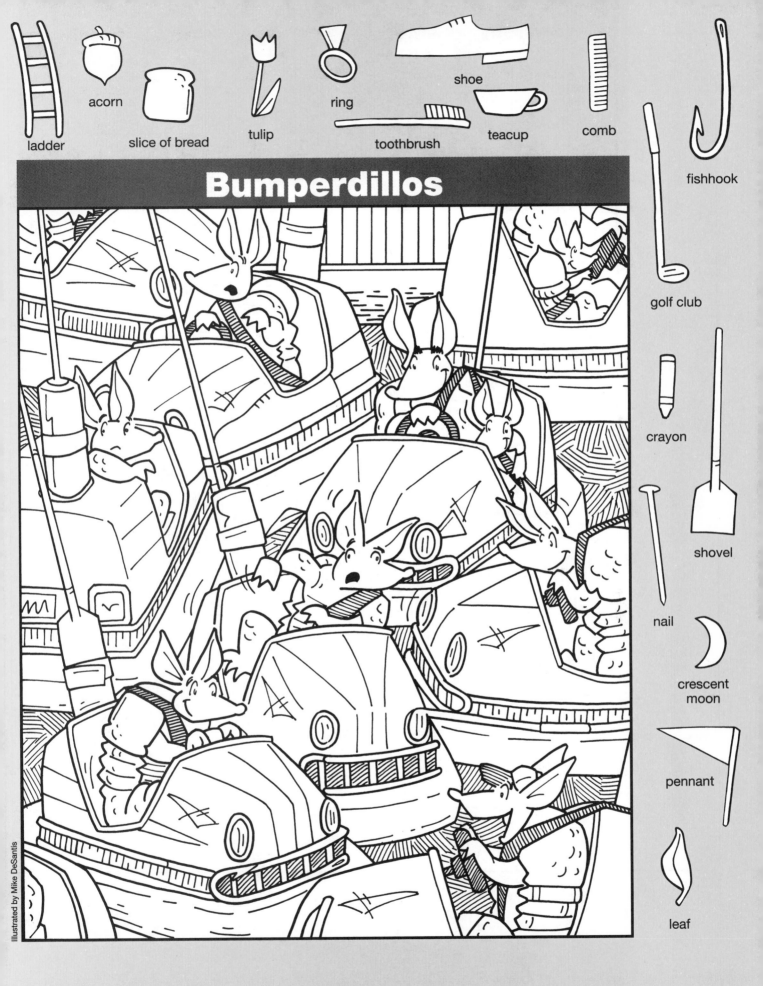

ladder
acorn
slice of bread
tulip
ring
shoe
toothbrush
teacup
comb
fishhook
golf club
crayon
shovel
nail
crescent moon
pennant
leaf

Illustrated by Mike DeSantis

At the Playground

pennant

nail

saw

caterpillar

crescent
moon

doughnut

comb

fishhook

envelope

harmonica

mallet

drinking straw

16

binoculars

button

boot

drumstick

belt

canoe

snake

pencil

crayon

slice of bread

slice of pie

ruler

Illustrated by Paul Richer

Bunny B-Ball

tack

spool of thread

butterfly

artist's brush

spoon

feather

button

carrot

slice of pie

banana

glove

spatula

bell

flying disk

ring

flashlight

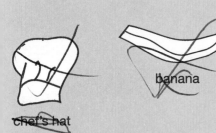
chef's hat

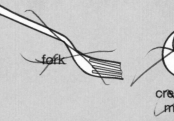
banana

mushroom

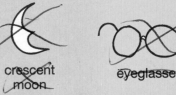
fork

crescent moon

eyeglasses

Heading Home

artist's brush

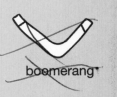
goose

boomerang

leaf

crayon

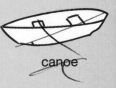
canoe

Get on Board

heart

carrot

bowling ball

golf club

broccoli

letter

wishbone

colander

magnet

lollipop

crown

belt

domino

button

slice of watermelon

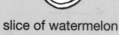
glove

spool of thread

football

doughnut

cookie

butterfly net

slice of watermelon

spool of thread

musical note

squirrel

ring

crescent moon

button

lollipop

book

needle

nail

high-heeled shoe

teacup

recorder

wishbone

Derby Day

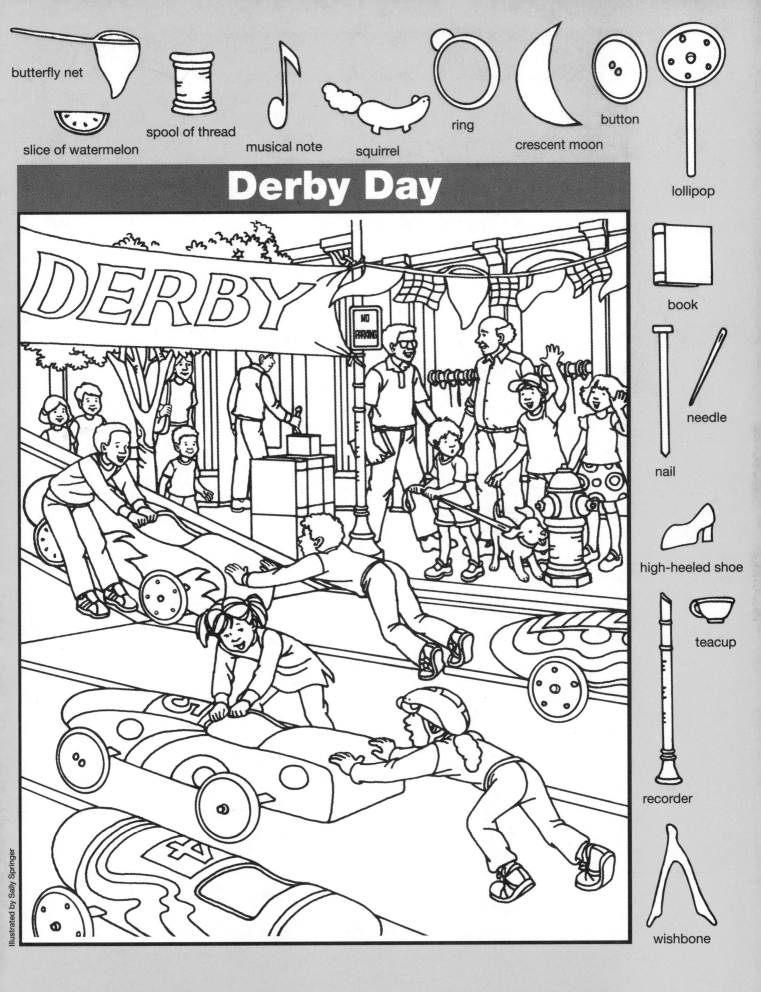

Illustrated by Sally Springer

21

Fall Chores

mitten

ring

paintbrush

mallet

funnel

mouse

mop

needle

mask

heart

mailbox

magnifying glass

crescent moon

mug

magnet

mushroom

lollipo

cupcake

milk carton

leaf

Illustrated by Olivia Cole

22

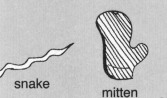
snake

mitten

snowman

slice of bacon

spoon

sock

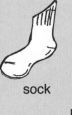
pencil

slice of pie

carrot

wristwatch

magnifying glass

bowl

bell

hammer

ruler

artist's brush

book

spatula

needle

Park Performance

SHOW TODAY!

Illustrated by Lyn Martin

Backyard Builders

boomerang

strawberry

butter knife

hockey stick

paper clip

crown

closed umbrella

fork

pencil

light bulb

artist's brush

toothbrush

slice of pizza

candle

Illustrated by Chuck Dillon

24

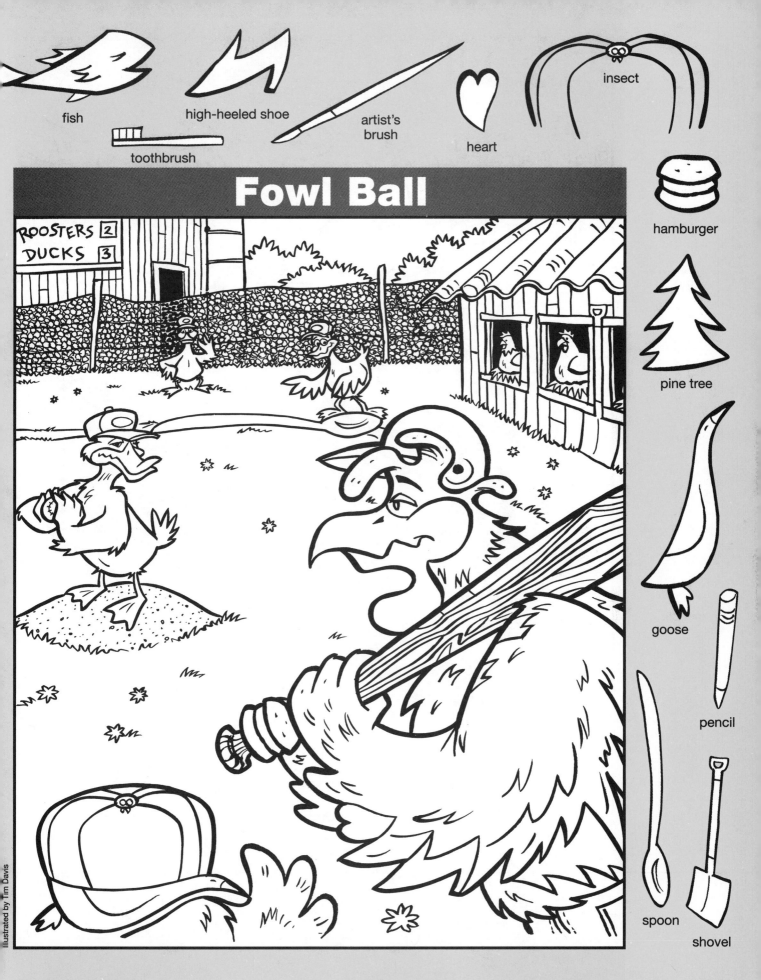

fish

high-heeled shoe

toothbrush

artist's brush

heart

insect

hamburger

pine tree

goose

pencil

spoon

shovel

Fowl Ball

ROOSTERS 2
DUCKS 3

Illustrated by Tim Davis

teacup

tube of
paint

pencil

candle

slice of
bread

butterfly

Friendly Race

spoon

banana

book

needle

apple core

slice of
cake

flower

shovel

ring

carrot

dustpan

artist's
brush

vase

paintbrush

pushpin

bell

flashlight

golf club

Illustrated by Charles Jordan

A Wild Time

candle

flag

needle

flyswatter

light bulb

boomerang

spoon

mallet

boot

banana

mug

bell

lollipop

wishbone

comb

Illustrated by Mary Sullivan

28

bat

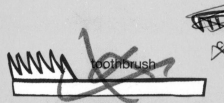
pair of pants

toothbrush

comb

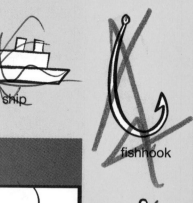
ship

fishhook

ring

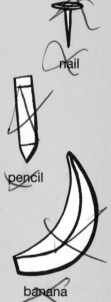
heart

nail

pencil

banana

ice-cream cone

Peanut Farmer

PEANUTS

hammer

flag

button

ice-cream bar

bottle

light bulb

golf club

jar

trowel

comb

hairbrush

fishhook

nail

flute

crescent moon

sock

safety

STOP

slice of pie

crescent moon

crown

pennant

nail

toothbrush

apple

flag

baseball cap

teacup

comb

heart

needle

mallet

fishhook

mushroom

ice-cream bar

spool of thread

snow cone

tack

lollipop

paintbrush

sailboat

Flying High

Illustrated by Olivia Cole

Tug o' War

banana

mushroom

fish

bowling
pin

pencil

can

book

loaf of bread

artist's
brush

flag

paintbrush

screwdriver

ball

slice of
lemon

handbell

caterpillar

candy cane

lollipop

tube of toothpaste

comb

slice of pizza

canoe

snake

letter

carrot

saw

acorn

Illustrated by Ron Zalme

Parade Day

boot

ring

hot dog

fish

paintbrush

screw

banana

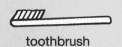
slice of bread

toothbrush

comb

slice of cake

drinking straw

pennant

34

tepee

teacup

nail

wedge of lemon

hot dog

shamrock

telescope

doughnut

candle

ring

heart

crescent moon

microphone

crown

lamp

fork

Gone Fishing

Illustrated by Marilee Harrald-Pilz

35

Johnny Appleseed

nail

arrow

banana

closed umbrella

needle

wishbone

tack

candle

golf club

pen

pennant

sailboat

crown

heart

spoon

question m

wishbone

muffin

carrot

flashlight

ear of corn

flag

lightning bolt

mushroom

olive

pliers

flower

mitten

heart

candle

Fly Fishing

Illustrated by Rocky Fuller

Sandlot Softball

ice-cream
cone

banana

paper clip

fish

pliers

elf's hat

pickax

boot

heart

spoon

candy
cane

teacup

bat

toothbrush

light bulb

Illustrated by Tim Davis

38

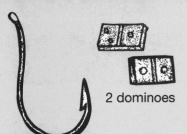 fishhook

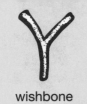 2 dominoes

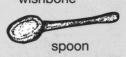 wishbone

 envelope

 snake

 doughnut

 spoon

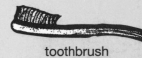 heart

toothbrush

 horseshoe

Message in a Bottle

 cane

 butterfly

 apple

 boomerang

 dragonfly

Illustrated by Arieh Zeldich

39

mug

flashlight

glove

pencil

crown

envelope

wedge of lemon

At the Dog Park

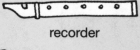
recorder

wishbone

bottle

heart

slice of pizza

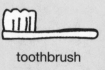
carrot

fork

toothbrush

banana

40

baseball bat

seashell

open book

paper clip

spoon

golf club

whale

cupcake

artist's brush

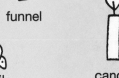
fish

snail

funnel

candle

crescent
moon

key

Illustrated by Maggie Swanson

41

The Peanut Pool

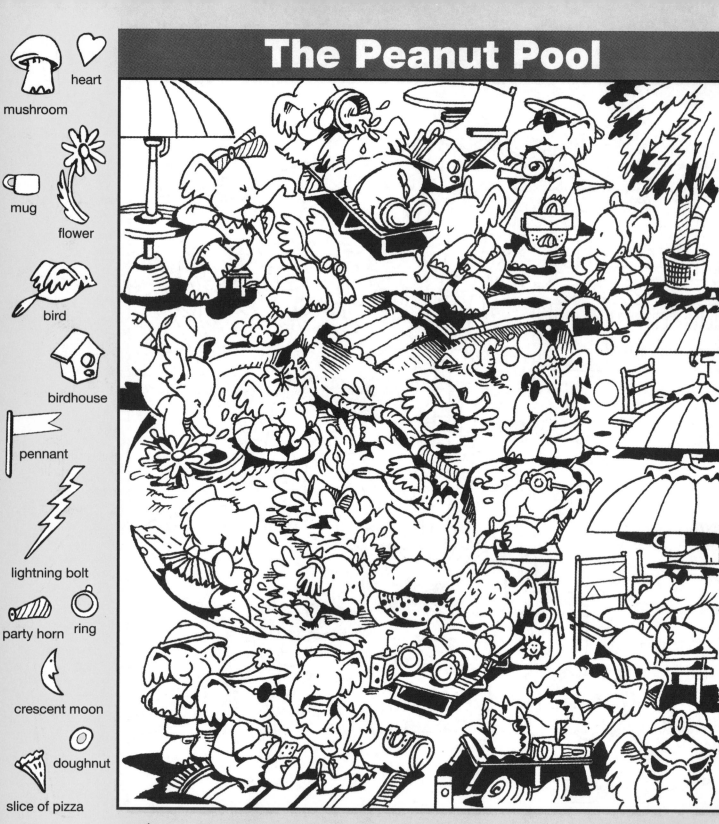

mushroom

heart

mug

flower

bird

birdhouse

pennant

lightning bolt

party horn

ring

crescent moon

doughnut

slice of pizza

bowl

artist's brush

horseshoe

peppermint stick

butterfly

envelope

piece of popcorn

glove

slice of bread

ice pop

lollipop

book

toothbrush

candle

baseball bat

flashlight

comb

fan

42

Illustrated by Diana Zourelias

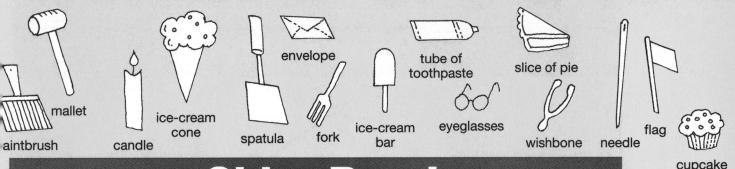

mallet

paintbrush

candle

ice-cream cone

spatula

fork

envelope

ice-cream bar

tube of toothpaste

eyeglasses

slice of pie

wishbone

needle

flag

cupcake

toothbrush

Cider Break

book

knitted hat

teacup

shoe

ring

slice of bread

cat

ladder

43

Hippo Dive

kite

magnifying
glass

key

crown

heart

gingerbread
cookie

eagle's head

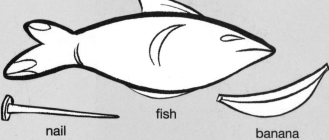

nail

fish

banana

eyeglasses

ruler

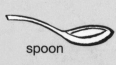

spoon

boomerang

boo

44

muffin

pointy hat

sailboat

needle

ruler

hedgehog

pencil

heart

mug

golf club

Painting Party

flag

screwdriver

envelope

bell

tent

nail

carrot

pennant

bow

eyeglasses

banana

slipper

coin purse

coffeepot

bugle

paintbrush

Playing Keep-Away

mop

high-heeled shoe

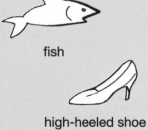

fish

pliers

hairbrush

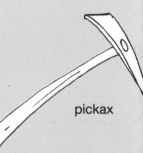

pickax

canoe

magnet

book

toothbrush

candle

nail

snake

pencil

heart

banana

Very Big Fish Tale

feather

glove

ice-cream cone

comb

Illustrated by Ron Lieser

Fish Lessons

ice-cream cone

pear

teapot

pencil

bird

saucepan

camera

dragonfly

spatula

butterfly

clock

whisk broom

crown

hamburg

48

bowl

acorn

magnifying glass

glove

clothespin

ice-cream cone

yardstick

pencil

pear

stopwatch

snake

fish

spoon

bell

needle

pine tree

dolphin

crayon

pennant

heart

pen

slice of cake

zipper

candle

horn

Walking the Dogs

Up and Away!

computer monitor

musical note

glove

spool of thread

candy cane

needle

football

can opener

spoon

crescent moon

sailboat

magnet

pencil

bunch of bananas

Illustrated by Rocky Fuller

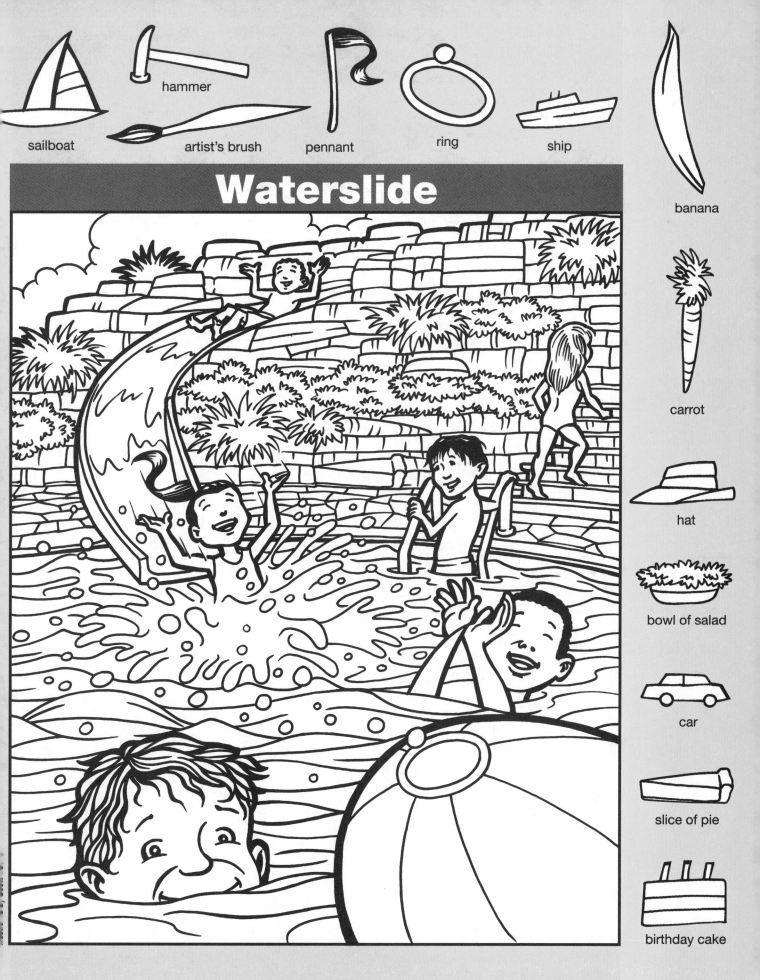

sailboat

hammer

artist's brush

pennant

ring

ship

banana

carrot

hat

bowl of salad

car

slice of pie

birthday cake

Waterslide

Wheeee!

candle

feather

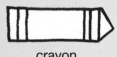

crayon

teacup

golf
club

radish

ice-cream cone

oilcan

mallet

ring

crown

nail

52

pushpin

artist's brush

slice of pie

pennant

pencil

bell

slice of pizza

slice of cake

flashlight

cupcake

mitten

spatula

Illustrated by Charles Jordan

53

Hula-Hoops

pie

banana

magnifying glass

candy cane

artist's brush

crown

book

belt

wedge of lemon

teacup

magnet

bell

snake

slice of pizza

lollipop

spoon

carrot

pennant

party hat

muffin

horseshoe

sailboat

caterpillar

kite

Illustrated by Lyn Martin

54

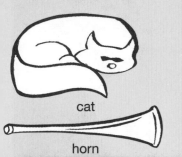
cat

horn

scissors

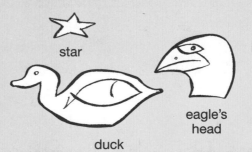
star

duck

eagle's head

sailboat

high-heeled shoe

toothbrush

bird

eyeglasses

pitcher

boot

Catching a Whale

Illustrated by Tim Davis

Picnic on the Pier

birthday cake

frying pan

butter knife

slice of watermelon

hat

domino

broccoli

artist's brush

pencil

LOBSTER ROLLS Yum Yum

LOBSTER DINNERS

Illustrated by Viki Woodworth

teacup

pennant

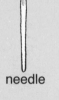
top hat

candy cane

needle

adhesive bandage

chicken

saucepan

hat

pitcher

button

needle

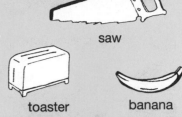
saw

toaster

banana

umbrella

The Bay Spa

saxophone

slice of bread

bow

light bulb

eyeglasses

headphones

sailboat

crown

artist's brush

golf club

sheep

boot

comb

apple

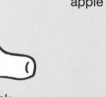
sock

musical note

screwdriver

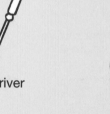
tack

needle

crayon

sponge
mop

cane

lollipop

hockey
stick

drinking
straw

Illustrated by R. Michael Palan

paintbrush

ice-cream cone

fish

toothbrush

nail

59

Duck Pond

umbrella

pitcher

light bulb

eyeglasses

crown

bunch of bananas

horn

iron

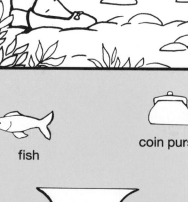

fish

coin purse

saltshaker

hat

bowl

high-heeled shoe

hammer

snail

Illustrated by Kathy Swain-O'Brien

ghost

domino

nail

snake

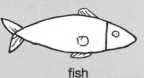
fish

pencil

Building a Snowman

slice of pizza

muffin

snow cone

cat's head

glove

mouse

61

Quiet, Please!

hoe

mug

mitten

party hat

boomerang

nail

paper clip

comb

needle

boot

sock

sailboat

ring

spool of thread

flute

slice of pizza

banana

toothbrush

muffin

game piece

party hat

golf club

Bird Patrol

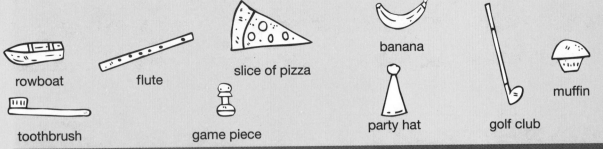

butter knife

mallet

pencil

sock

fishhook

pennant

Coastal Birding Area

Illustrated by Mary Sullivan

radish

hatchet

teacup

slice of pie

carrot

ice-cream
cone

sailboat

crayon

bowl

ring

trowel

spoon

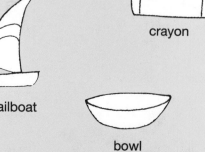

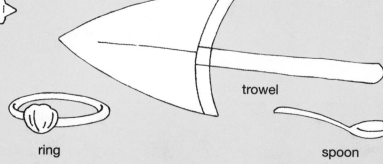

candle

handbell

nail

pickax

tack

fish

mushroom

lollipop

banana

wooden shoe

elf's hat

Illustrated by Lynn Adams

65

Penguin Hoops

bell

deer

canoe

egg

book

glove

eagle's head

crown

star

horn

banana

heart

duck

Illustrated by Tim Davis

chef's hat

broccoli

cat's head

lizard

paper clip

fishhook

paintbrush

baseball bat

envelope

star

pennant

pencil

rabbit

Berry Delicious

Illustrated by Dani Jones

Juicy Oranges

turtle

ring

tube of toothpaste

fish

spoon

teacup

artist's brush

worm

crescent moon

envelope

mushroom

Illustrated by R. Michael Palan

toothbrush

cupcake

pencil

pennant

needle

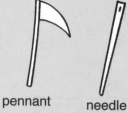
screwdriver

flashlight

nail

68

mushroom

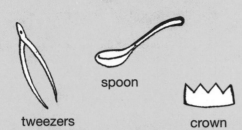 spoon

tweezers

 crown

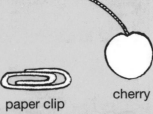 bell

paper clip

cherry

 cane

 light bulb

Free Ride

 snake

 scrub brush

 toothbrush

 lollipop

 tack

 paintbrush

Picnic in the Park

flashlight

artist's brush

key

heart

spatula

seashell

carrot

spool of thread

pushpin

wishbone

shoe

light bulb

mitten

slice of bread

crescent moon

safety pin

glove

baseball bat

screwdriver

clothespin

Illustrated by Maggie Swanson

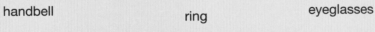

fish

handbell

dog bone

ring

eyeglasses

toothbrush

Pool Safety

envelope

kite

banana

snake

pencil

candle

spider

crown

spoon

button

toothbrush

plate

Illustrated by David Helton

candle
wishbone
light bulb
bowling pin
teacup
crayon
heart
needle
spool of thread
glove
baseball bat
ruler
spoon
nail
toothbrush
envelope
pitcher

Game of Jacks

Blueberry Season

balloon

candy cane

needle

funnel

paper clip

carrot

fish

tennis
ball

eyeglasses

ice-cream bar

spoon

sailboat

artist's
brush

Illustrated by Rocky Fuller

74

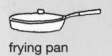
frying pan

spool of thread

safety pin

carrot

telescope

book

ice-cream cone

Hockey on the Pond

pushpin

shovel

funnel

candle

slice of cake

Into the Wind

carrot

banana

hoe

party hat

cupcake

hockey stick

duck

ring

spoon

tepee

frying pan

teacup

flashlight

needle

Illustrated by Karen Stormer Brooks

 yo-yo

slice of pizza

paper clip

bell

fried egg

fishhook

 bowl

acorn

shovel

 kite

 hockey stick

pail

 yardstick

oilcan

 toothbrush

 candle

Rainy-Day Dance

Burying His Bone

crown

ice-cream cone

paper clip

pencil

T-shirt

banana

bell

eyeglasses

heart

squirrel

glove

mushroom

bird

feather

fish

spoo

ring

slice of cake

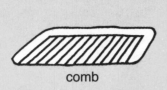
comb

flag

drinking straw

nail

needle

cotton candy

screw

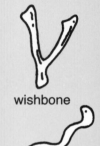
wishbone

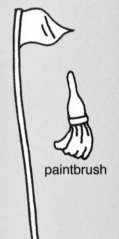
snake

pennant

paintbrush

spool of thread

teacup

Double Dutch

A Hot Idea!

umbrella

sailboat

pencil

wishbone

drinking
straw

ice-cream
bar

sock

acorn

candle

pear

clothespin

arrow

book

needle

slice of pizza

pennant

ring

nail

toothbrush

bowl

mug

comb

crescent moon

ruler

ice-cream cone

musical note

envelope

fishhook

Illustrated by Sally Springer

81

Strike One

key

ice-cream cone

bell

horseshoe

banana

frog

pencil

toothbrush

duck

sailboat

comb

saw

fish

book

in-line skate

heart

bowling

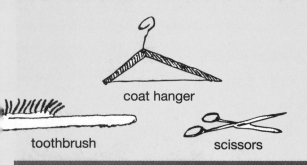
toothbrush

coat hanger

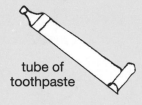
scissors

tube of
toothpaste

fishhook

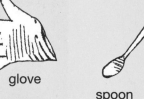
glove

spoon

mallet

nail

comb

ring

pencil

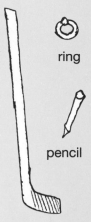
hockey
stick

clothespin

roller skate

Match Point

Illustrated by Valeri Gorbachev

Coming Down

check mark

needle

teacup

tack

handbell

arrow

wedge of cheese

crown

feather

telescope

mitten

spool of thread

fishhoo

Illustrated by Rocky Fuller

84

chicken

ring

heart

banana

paper clip

toothbrush

party horn

sailboat

crown

bell

Close Encounter

pencil

saw

feather

light bulb

book

illustrated by Tim Davis

85

Pick Your Own Apples

bowl

hat

snake

crown

candle

pennant

flashlight

sock

carrot

crescent moon

fishhook

mushroom

heart

cat's head

sailboat

slice of pizza

slice of pie

two shoes

chicken

needle

teacup

fish

ice-cream cone

nail

tack

spoon

Illustrated by Olivia Cole

86

shoe
pear
bell
cotton candy
wristwatch
ring
wishbone
envelope
eyeglasses
sock
teacup
mitten
pennant
dart
crescent moon
slice of pizza
four-leaf clover

slice of cake

wrench

needle
arrow
olive
pencil
artist's brush
peppermint stick
ax
carrot
candle
heart
bowl

S'mores for All!

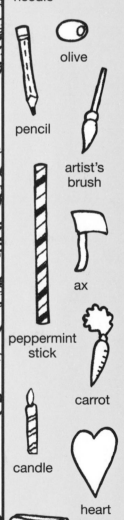

Illustrated by Diana Zourelias

The Snowflake

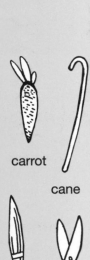
carrot

cane

artist's brush

scissors

pennant

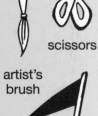
comb

lollipop

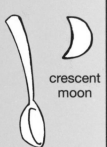
crescent moon

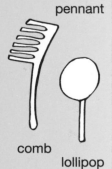
spoon

musical note

cupcake

crown

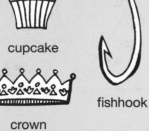
fishhook

paintbrush

candle

slice of watermelon

toothbrush

bell

ring

88

Illustrated by Maxim Mitrofanov

cotton candy

nail

question mark

slice of pie

needle

heart

bird

party hat

toothbrush

fishhook

cane

golf club

crescent moon

flag

artist's brush

Surfing School

illustrated by Sally Springer

89

Soccer Kick

teacup

bell

pencil

heart

feather

shovel

ice-cream cone

star

ruler

horn

fish

dog

crown

90

Illustrated by Tim Davis

muffin

comb

button

wishbone

artist's brush

shuttlecock

bowl

hammer

drinking straw

pencil

crown

candle

glove

Field Trip

NATURE TRAIL

Riding Camp

saw

seashell

clothespin

baseball bat

paintbrush

mitten

mug

shoe

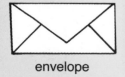
envelope

cherries

carrot

ring

spoon

pencil

canoe

light bulb

can

screwdriver

slice of pizza

open book

screw

artist's brush

ice-cream cone

rabbit

key

fork

crown

lemon

acorn

banana

candle

broccoli

heart

star

fish

Illustrated by Maggie Swanson

93

Car Wash

feather

spoon

ice-cream cone

heart

banana

sneaker

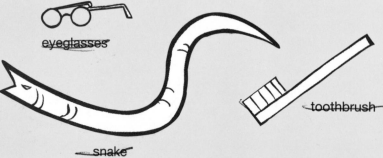

eyeglasses

snake

toothbrush

hat

mitten

megapho

Illustrated by Tim Davis

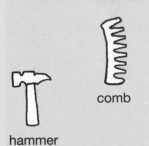
hammer

comb

sheep

handbell

mouse

seal

candle

It's Snowing! We're Skiing!

pencil

scissors

spoon

horn

fish

baseball
bat

Illustrated by R. Michael Palan

95

Dog Show

banana

ice-cream cone

doughnut

spoon

wishbone

muffin

lollipop

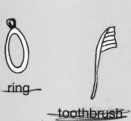
ring

toothbrush

feather

glove

pencil

snake

ladder

heart

Illustrated by Barbara Emmons

96

heart

bat

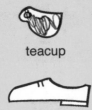
mitten

teacup

shoe

wishbone

spoon

sock

crescent moon

banana

pencil

Piggy Pyramid

artist's brush

crown

coffeepot

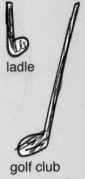
ladle

golf club

button

crayon

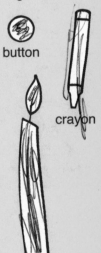
candle

Illustrated by Mike DeSantis

97

Eight-Armed Surprise

bird

coin

toothbrush

glove

eyeglasses

wedge of cheese

hourglass

bell

ring

spoon

eagle's head

teacup

mouse

Illustrated by Tim Davis

banana

candle

shoe

toothbrush

spoon

pennant

ice-cream cone

lollipop

glove

hockey stick

bowl

paintbrush

crayon

lamp

Tents Up

Illustrated by Mary Sullivan

Cabbage Patch

mushroom

boomerang

pinwheel

needle

artist's brush

carrot

wishbone

straight pin

comb

crescent moon

goose

hanger

worm

domino

spatula

Illustrated by Lynn Adams

Watering the Flowers

starfish

fishhook

teacup

musical note

toothbrush

ruler

banana

fish

crown

closed umbrella

ring

sailboat

button

pencil

ice-cream cone

heart

baseball cap

muffin

glove

envelope

scissors

bell

needle

Illustrated by Laura Freeman

101

Hot Drinks

Hot Chocolate and Hot Cider

handbell

pennant

bowl

ghost

candle

toothbrush

sailboat

cap

trowel

slice of pie

whale

carrot

pitcher

crayon

Illustrated by Janet Robertson

102

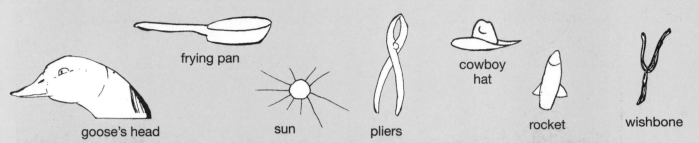

frying pan

goose's head

sun

pliers

cowboy hat

rocket

wishbone

Pleasant Pastimes

parrot

loaf of bread

horse's head

bird

musical notes

mushroom

Illustrated by Milj Colson-Barnum

103

wedge of orange

sock

needle

open book

telephone receiver

celery

ladder

party hat

banana

rabbit

snake

apple

horseshoe

ladle

Illustrated by Karen Stormer Brooks

104

funnel

bug

heart

dress

flashlight

snake

bowl

bell

tack

drinking glass

lampshade

toothbrush

screwdriver

mug

Soccer Knights

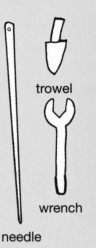

trowel

wrench

needle

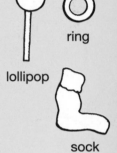

saw

ring

lollipop

sock

ice-cream cone

artist's brush

saucepan

Illustrated by Larry Daste

105

wishbone

funnel

toothbrush

hamburger

saltshaker

baseball glove

High-Rise Garden

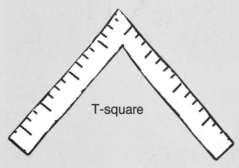

T-square

ice-cream
cone

hairbrush

slice of pie

106

heart

gingerbread man

bell

artist's brush

light bulb

spoon

Illustrated by John Nez

flashlight

doughnut

tube of
toothpaste

slice of pizza

squeeze bottle

croquet
mallet

107

Rad Rabbits

candle

egg

crescent moon

pinecone

crayon

mushroom

jelly bean

baseball bat

hot-dog bun

flag

heart

fish

nail

wishbone

bell

slice of pie

canoe

feather

Illustrated by Gary Mohrman

bat

spoon

whistle

candle

tack

clothespin

acorn

fork

sock

slice of pie

needle

boomerang

feather

nail

bird

elf's hat

Mouse House

109

Everybody Skate!

crescent moon

kite

screwdriver

doughnut

fork

pennant

cherry

artist's brush

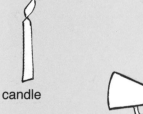
candle

megaphone

banana

starfish

safety pin

flower

slice of bread

comb

butterfly

heart

leaf

nail

needle

snake

bell

pine tree

crown

clover

sailboat

envelope

Illustrated by Ellen Appleby

111

pennant

pushpin

fishhook

hedgehog

egg

cherry

golf club

tennis ball

football

tack

crescent moon

key

heart

bat

dolphin

slice of
watermelon

tennis ball

cotton swab

slice of
orange

snake

banana

open book

Swim Team

sailboat

ring

doughnut

crescent
moon

pencil

toothbrush

illustrated by Jane Ramsey

Basketful of Spots

ring

canoe

heart

horseshoe

hamburger

saltshaker

book

rabbit

butterfly

2 birds

mushroom

tepee

eyeglasses

coffeepot

snake

whale

crescent moon

pe

snail

light bulb

butterfly

mushroom

wishbone

pennant

bowl

trowel

shirt

slice of pie

muffin

glove

Mole Swimming Hole

hairpin

needle

nail

ice-cream
cone

spoon

letter

2 candles

crescent moon

Butterfly Habitat

slice of bread

wedge of lemon

artist's brush

dog bone

fork

mug

rabbit

ice-cream cone

glove

baseball bat

fish

mushroom

slice of pizza

candle

shoe

pen

key

crown

116

sailboat

fried egg

spoon

mitten

banana

button

star

seal

heart

envelope

Illustrated by Maggie Swanson

pcake

light bulb

crescent moon

ring

car

carrot

handbell

bat

117

Loading Pumpkins

slice of cake

banana

nail

pencil

crayon

ballpoint pen

closed umbrella

ice-cream bar

mushroom

magic wand

golf club

candl

Illustrated by Charles Jordan

118

frying pan

spoon

ring

toothbrush

handbag

funnel

heart

hat

banana

artist's brush

lollipop

rabbit

nail

needle

candle

tweezers

mitten

pennant

hatchet

crescent moon

Ollie's Garden

KELP

Illustrated by Karen Stormer Brooks

119

scissors

hammer

heart

2 birds

whale

baseball glove

artist's brush

fish

needle

chef's hat

potato

Bumper Crop

Illustrated by Shawn Berlute-Shea

doughnut

peach

safety pin

slice of
bread

wishbone

toothbrush

fishhook

122

carrot

pear

teacup

slice of pizza

banana

muffin

spoon

key

musical note

heart

bowling ball

high-heeled shoe

golf club

fork

cherry

drumstick

shoe

Illustrated by Jim Fitzgerald

Apple Tree

closed umbrella

Illustrated by Charles Jordan

slice of cake

candle

safety pin

teacup

pushpin

slice of pie

feather

bell

golf club

mitten

open book

elf's hat

sheep's head

light bulb

cat

glove

hot dog

pie

bird

swan

Winter Sports

Illustrated by Mii Colson-Barnum

hockey stick

heart

spoon

turtle

rabbit

elf's head

shamrock

Giant Sunflowers

pencil

wishbone

banana

hot dog

worm

pine tree

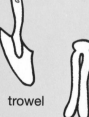

trowel

clothespin

shoe

crescent moon

nail

sock

fishhook

Illustrated by R. Michael Palan

126

pig

open book

key

comb

squirrel

pencil

light bulb

toothbrush

Bunny Slope

carrot

pliers

shoe

fan

shark

sailboat

sock

Illustrated by Leslie Franz

127

golf club

tube of toothpaste

open book

muffin

crayon

ice-cream cone

artist's brush

hairbrush

candle

fishhook

wedge of cheese

ballpoint pen

carrot

jar

slice of
pie

musical
note

mug

toothbrush

Illustrated by Charles Jordan

slice of
bread

spatula

spoon

pushpin

slice of cake

screwdriver

pencil

129

Answers

▼ Pages 4–5

▼ Page 6

▼ Page 7

▼ Page 8

▼ Page 9

▼ Pages 10–11

▼ Page 12

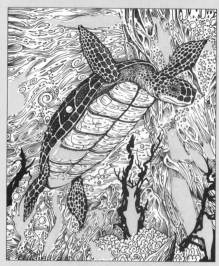

Answers

▼ Page 13

▼ Page 14

▼ Page 15

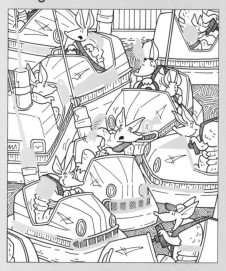

▼ Pages 16–17

▼ Page 18

▼ Page 19

▼ Page 20

▼ Page 21

Answers

▼Page 22

▼Page 23

▼Page 24

▼Page 25

▼Pages 26–27

▼Page 28

▼Page 29

▼Page 30

▼ Page 31

▼ Pages 32–33

▼ Page 34

▼ Page 35

▼ Page 36

▼ Page 37

▼ Page 38

▼ Page 39

Answers

▼ Pages 40–41

▼ Page 42

▼ Page 43

▼ Page 44

▼ Page 45

▼ Page 46

▼ Page 47

▼ Page 48

Answers

▼ Page 49

▼ Page 50

▼ Page 51

▼ Pages 52–53

▼ Page 54

▼ Page 55

▼ Page 56

▼ Page 57

Answers

▼Pages 58–59

▼Page 60

▼Page 61

▼Page 62

▼Page 63

▼Pages 64–65

▼Page 66

▼ Page 67

▼ Page 68

▼ Page 69

▼ Pages 70–71

▼ Page 72

▼ Page 73

▼ Page 74

▼ Page 75

Answers

▼ Page 76

▼ Page 77

▼ Page 78

▼ Page 79

▼ Pages 80–81

▼ Page 82

▼ Page 83

▼ Page 84

Answers

▼ Page 85

▼ Page 86

▼ Page 87

▼ Page 88

▼ Page 89

▼ Page 90

▼ Page 91

▼ Pages 92–93

Answers

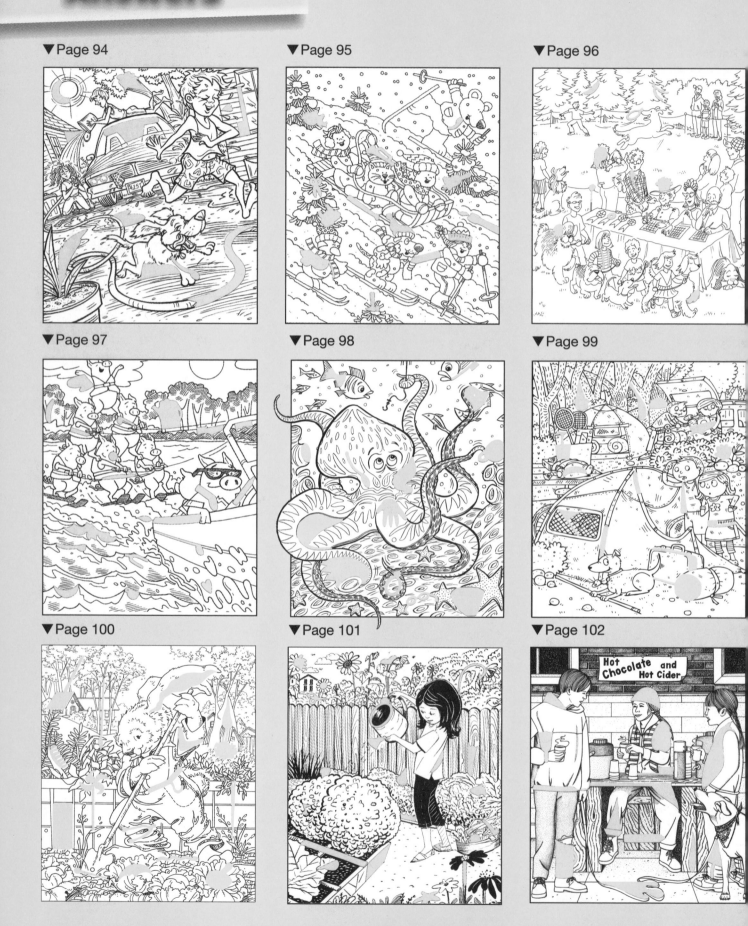

▼Page 94

▼Page 95

▼Page 96

▼Page 97

▼Page 98

▼Page 99

▼Page 100

▼Page 101

▼Page 102

Answers

▼ Page 103

▼ Page 104

▼ Page 105

▼ Pages 106–107

▼ Page 108

▼ Page 109

▼ Pages 110–111

Answers

▼ Page 112

▼ Page 113

▼ Page 114

▼ Page 115

▼ Pages 116–117

▼ Page 118

▼ Page 119

Answers

▼Page 120

▼Page 121

Pages 122–123

▼Page 124

Page 125

▼Page 126

▼Page 127

Answers

▼Pages 128-129

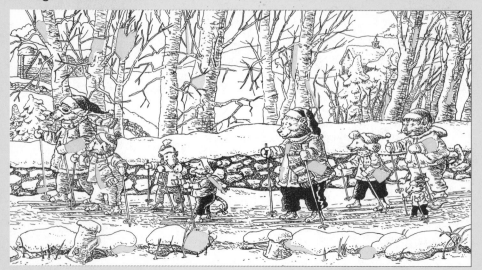